# THAT WAS 1949

MARK JONES

Copyright © 2019 Mark Jones

All rights reserved.

*There's a power of good for you in HALL'S WINE*

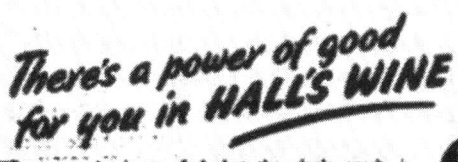

When you begin to feel that the day's work is getting you down; when your spirits sink and the jobs pile up ahead of you — it's wonderful what real good a glass of Hall's Wine will do you; and how good it tastes, too!

## HALL'S WINE

Reduced price : Large bottle 12/-

REPRESENTATIVES FOR EIRE : A. MILLAR & CO. LTD. 10 13 THOMAS ST., DUBLIN
Guaranteed by the Proprietors, Stephen Smith & Co. Ltd., London, E.3

(a5299-6)

**CONTENTS**

January – 7

February - 13

March – 19

April – 25

May – 31

June - 37

July - 43

August - 47

September – 53

October - 57

November - 61

December - 65

# HELP TO FORM YOUR NEW TERRITORIAL UNIT

112 CONTROL & REPORT DETACHMENT, R.A. (T.A.) ATTACHED TO R.A.F. REQUIRES OFFICERS FOR LIAISON BETWEEN R.A.F. AND A.A. ARTILLERY.

GIRLS TO OPERATE COMMUNICATIONS

PAYMENT FOR ALL DRILLS PLUS YEARLY BOUNTY £8

Apply **DRILL HALL, The Goffs,** TEL. 1597 **Eastbourne.**

## HELP KEEP THE PEACE

# Look at your RENT BOOK!

and consider that for almost the same weekly outlay you could BUY your house and provide for the future security of your family and yourself

*then ask your landlord if he will sell!*

Particulars of financial assistance available to help you to purchase will be given without obligation by the

**Systematic Saving in SUBSCRIPTION SHARES at 2¾% Tax Paid** may be the first step to the owning of your own home. Ask for details.

## LEEDS PERMANENT
### BUILDING SOCIETY

Look! Smarts

DOUBLE LUCKY

furniture SALE

# JANUARY

THE YEAR started with many roads throughout Britain icebound and dangerous, as further falls of snow were reported by patrols in North Staffordshire, at Macclesfield and areas of Northamptonshire. In Lincolnshire, it had been falling for 12 hours. A belt of rain enveloped practically the whole of the south of England after a continual rise in temperature. In the Midlands the expected snow arrived but the falls were not very heavy. The weather didn't stop Prince Charles making his first journey, when Princess Elizabeth and the Duke of Edinburgh took him from Buckingham Palace to Sandringham.

At least 40 people were killed and 400 injured when tornado crushed part of the small lumber town of Warron in Arkansas, USA. Mayor Jim Hurley said on January 4th that damage was least £250,000. Fires, which broke out after the tornado, were a serious menace because water supplies had been cut. Witnesses said the tornado swept through the town with the noise express train. Rescuers were searching the scattered debris left by the "twister" for other victims.

The King Denmark said that he has a 'dream wife' and that his three Princess daughters are delightful—

-"although you sometimes feel like choking them for their tom foolery". The King made these outright statements in a broadcast on January 12th for children from the royal Castle. That same day, three men were killed when an American plane on the Berlin air lift crashed while returning unloaded from Berlin through light snow. The plane cut swathe yards long through forest.

The Minister in charge of the American Economic Co-operation Administration mission to the United Kingdom, told the Manchester Chamber of Commerce: "The gains British production and exports have been highly satisfactory. The campaign for economic recovery in Britain is one of the greatest national efforts ever seen in a time of peace."

On January 19th, ten U.S. Coastguardsmen were killed and scores burned and injured in a collision between two American ships in a fog off the New

Jersey coast. The vessels were the 3.000-ton cutter *Eastwind* and the 10,195-ton tanker *Gulf Stream*. The Boston Coastguard said the report of the collision was radioed by the cutter's captain.

Meanwhile, Sabotage was not being overlooked as a possible cause of the disappearance of the *British South American Airways* Tudor IV *Star Ariel* between Bermuda and Kingston, Jamaica. The airliner was the second Tudor IV to be lost without trace in the South Atlantic and within two hours flying of Bermuda. Lord Pakenham. Minister of Civil Aviation, told the House of Lords on January 20th that *British South American Airways* had decided suspend Tudor IV's from service pending special investigation of each individual aircraft. He announced that the *Star Ariel* must be presumed lost and said that there was little hope for the survival of the airliner's 13 passengers and seven crew members.

That same day, Harry S. Truman took the solemn oath of office as 32nd President of the United States. For the first time, the inaugural ceremonies were shown by television to an audience estimated at ten millions from the Atlantic coast to the mid-west. Approximately 800 radio stations broadcast the President's address, and more than 750.000 visitors came to Washington to witness—or try to witness—the inauguration and took part in the festivities marking this most elaborate and expensive Inauguration Week in United States history.

> Many of the services supplied by the Westminster Bank cost the user little or nothing. Yet all of them help, in one way or another, to make life a little easier. Ask the Manager of your local branch about Travellers' Cheques, Bankers' Orders, and the Joint Account
>
> **WESTMINSTER BANK**
> LIMITED

General Chiang Kai Shek, President of China, leader of the Nationalists, and virtual Dictator for twenty years resigned and quitted the Communist-pressed capital of Nanking. He said before he left his capital, that he was departing because the Communists had not stopped fighting in answer to his New Year peace appeal. And so the first major nation is falling to the renewed wave of Communism, and the Republic of China is slowly nearing its end as the Reds swarm over the country.

Back in Europe, Russian blockade measures were likened to "movements of the boa constrictor" in a British official booklet released on January 21st. "Notes on the Blockade of Berlin, 1948," said the British community was "very much alive, busy and on the job. The 85-page booklet blamed the Russians for Berliners' present difficulties. Meanwhile, relatives crowded into the offices of the German welfare authorities in Berlin seeking news of a British airlift Dakota which crashed just inside the Soviet zone. There were 27 people on board, including five children and 14 Women. The passengers were sick people and undernourished children being flown out of Berlin the British zone.

On January 25th, Israeli and Egyptian delegations at the Rhodes armistice talks sent special Envoys home to consult with their Governments. Informal meetings –would later take place on the return of those envoys that left for Tel Aviv and Cairo.

In the USA, Walter Gieseking, the German pianist, was detained by immigration officers, shortly before the first concert of his American tour was to begin. The Department of Justice had announced the cancellation Gieseking's tour shortly before people arriving at Carnegie Hall, New York, for a concert found Jewish war veterans and other people picketing the hall. Police stopped several scuffles. Gieseking was warned on arrival that his admissibility was in doubt, a Justice Department spokesman said. All 2,700 tickets for the recital were sold-out.

In the UK, Princess Elizabeth was suffering from an attack of measles, which was taking an ordinary course. The Princess was at Sandringham. She was being attended by Dr J. N. B. Ansell. The King and Queen, who were in residence at Sandringham, were at once informed of Princess Elizabeth's illness. Although measles is infectious for several days before the rash appears, it was considered very unlikely that Prince Charles would catch the infection from his mother. A British Medical Association spokesman said: "cases of measles are very rare for a baby of that age." Prince Charles was just over two months old.

# FEBRUARY

The first ship to arrive in Britain from the Antarctic whaling fleets arrived at Liverpool. The ship was loaded with a £1,000,000 cargo, including whale oil for Britain's fat ration. A quantity of whale meat was to be used for cattle food, whilst a sample consignment was canned in the Antarctic for the first time.

On January 7th, Hitler's Chancellery, which took two years to build, was almost completely destroyed in two minutes by a series of explosions. Only the massive outer walls and the balcony, from which Hitler addressed huge Party rallies, were left standing. Soviet-controlled German police, carrying small red flags, cordoned off all streets leading to the Chancellery.

In London, scientists from six nations began a conference to consider the progress made in research, and the new drug called antrycide. Antrycide, it was believed, would have far reaching results in the extermination of sleeping sickness prevalent among cattle in African territories.

Cardinal Mindszenty, Primate of Hungary, was sentenced to life imprisonment at Budapest on January 8th, a week after a 'people's republic' was declared in the country. All his private property was ordered to be confiscated. He was found guilty of three charges: —(1) Violating the law for the defence of the Republic; (2) organising conspiracy against the Republic; and (3) treason and black-market currency dealings. One report noted that: "Cardinal Mindszenty impassively stood' with folded hands as he listened to the verdicts. He had pleaded guilty to the acts charged, but denied treason".

*She's walking on air in a new pair of*
# BOOFERS

On February 10th, the film star Robert Mitchum (31), was sentenced to 60 days in prison in Los Angeles on a charge of conspiracy to possess marijuana cigarettes. Lila Leeds (20), the actress, convicted with Mitchum on the marijuana possession charges was also given 60 days' imprisonment. The judge placed Mitchum on probation for two years. Mitchum's lawyer said: "This was not due to a desire or habit as to marijuana but was rather due to association and seeking what you might call local colour."

> **BEER IS BEST**
>
> in the home-like atmosphere
>
> that is true to the
>
> ancient traditions of the inn

At the end of the month, figures showed that road deaths in Great Britain during February totalled 356, compared with 402 in January and 305 in the corresponding month. In addition 10,353 persons' were injured, 2,663 of them seriously. Of 4,013 accidents attributed to drivers, motor cyclists, and pedal cyclists, the biggest single cause was turning right without due care.

Major- General G. K. Bourne, the British Commandant in Berlin, banned the film "Oliver Twist," which caused Jewish riots in the city, after instructing Mr. Henry Durban, the J. Arthur Rank representative in Berlin, not to show the film again, "publicly or privately." Leaders of the Jewish community wanted to see "Oliver Twist" after Rabbi Schwartzschild had said that the Jewish community had behaved unreasonably, that there was nothing anti-Semitic in the film, and that it was, in his opinion, good entertainment. He also appealed to members of the Jewish faith to behave reasonably.

An Indian was killed in a clash Durban on January 21st, when crowds of Africans attacked Indian bus and motor cars. Other Indians were wounded. Many were sent to hospital. Police said that an African was shot from Indian motor car and wounded. The driver of an Indian bus was pulled from his cab and stabbed. He died from his injuries. The bus was set afire. Many arrests were made. News of the fighting spread quickly, and hundreds of angry Africans made a mass assault the district, pelting Indian cars with stones.

On February 24th, Jews and Egyptians ended nine months strife in Palestine. They signed a general armistice agreement ruling out "any warlike or hostile act' between their forces. The agreement laid down that the demarcation line agreed between the two parties was not to be constructed in any sense as a Political or territorial boundary. The line, the agreement said, was "delineated without prejudice to rights, claims, and positions of either party to the armistice as regards ultimate settlement of the Palestine question."

As the month drew to a close, news of a 2000-year-old tattooed mummy, preserved by the freezing temperatures, made the headlines. It had been discovered by a Russian archaeologist in the Altai Mountains, according to the Russian Academy of Sciences. He was believed to have been a prince or a tribal chief. Articles his tomb included a magnificent chariot, which was probably his hearse, and leather carpets, wooden animals, bronze mirrors, jewellery and furs.

Butlin's
LUXURY
HOLIDAY CAMPS
FOR THE
HOLIDAY OF
YOUR CHOICE
FOR FREE BOOKLET write to Butlin's
Ltd., 439, Oxford Street, London, W.1.

# MARCH

A CUT of two-pence in the value of the weekly meat ration was forecast by the meat trade. Stocks of corned beef were running low, but it was expected the weekly two-pence worth of corned beef will be continued. A Ministry of Food official of the *Whale Meat Advisory Bureau* said: "The shortage of meat is now so acute that it must be supplemented from other sources. Canning of whale meat already proceeding, and this will to come extent make the shortage". A spokesman confirmed that British ships were on their way back from the Antarctic with approximately 5,000 tons. The Ministry of Food expressed hope that the "public will gradually take to it, but everything depends on how it is marketed. If it is handled in a hygienic way, and is in first-class condition, there should be a demand for it". Meanwhile, talks were underway between British and French officials regarding the possibility of importing carcase meat from-France. It was hoped to get supplies of beef and pork. One of the main questions raised by the British authorities was the danger of introducing foot-and-mouth disease to the UK.

By mid-March, the British Minister of Health, Aneurin Bevan, said he was prepared to pay leading specialists who took full-time work under the new

National Health Service up to £5250 a year, with equal pay for men and women. Regional hospital boards, boards of governors of teaching hospitals, and the medical and dental professions received from Bevan the proposed terms and conditions of service for hospital, medical and dental staffs.

**MORE POWER IN THE new "CATERPILLAR" D.4**

Does the same job in less time or a bigger job in the same time.

**MAKES YOUR WORK FASTER, EASIER, CHEAPER**

It was reported that at least 200,000 German prisoners of war were still in Russia. A Note handed to the Soviet Government by the British Ambassador in Moscow asked why they have been retained. The United States also sent a Note to the Soviets dealing with the failure to repatriate Germans.

In London, on March 17th, the King passed a quiet night, and was continuing to make satisfactory progress after doctors were ordered to the Palace, but no bulletin was issued. Meanwhile, an appeal for an additional petrol allowance for motorists for Easter was made in the Commons. The Parliamentary

Secretary of the Fuel Ministry replied: "I might be forthright at the beginning and say, very plainly, there cannot be any extra, petrol for Easter this year."

A 41-year-old woman whose hair was said to have stood up on end like bristles after visit to a hairdresser won her claim for damages. She was awarded a total of £300 against the hairdresser. Cecily Smith claimed against Constance Stevens, by whom she was given a 'perm' in June 1945. The plaintiff said she was left unattended for 15 minutes and the 'cooker' became overheated. The state of her hair afterwards drove her to hysteria. The judge said the perm 'was not carried out with that degree of skill which a person had right to expect'.

Oswald Mosley's Union Movement was not allowed to stage another London march for at least three months—probably longer after an incident which involved clashes, injuries and arrests. The Home Secretary issued an order prohibiting all political processions in the Metropolitan police district for three months. "I regret it is necessary to take this step, but it is intolerable that the streets of our metropolis should be made a battleground for opposing factions," he said.

Meanwhile, Britain moved still nearer to balancing her trade with the rest of the world. Figures showed that the gap between what we buy and what we sell abroad was down to £16.million. Britain exported more coal, but fewer cars, and less food, drink and tobacco.

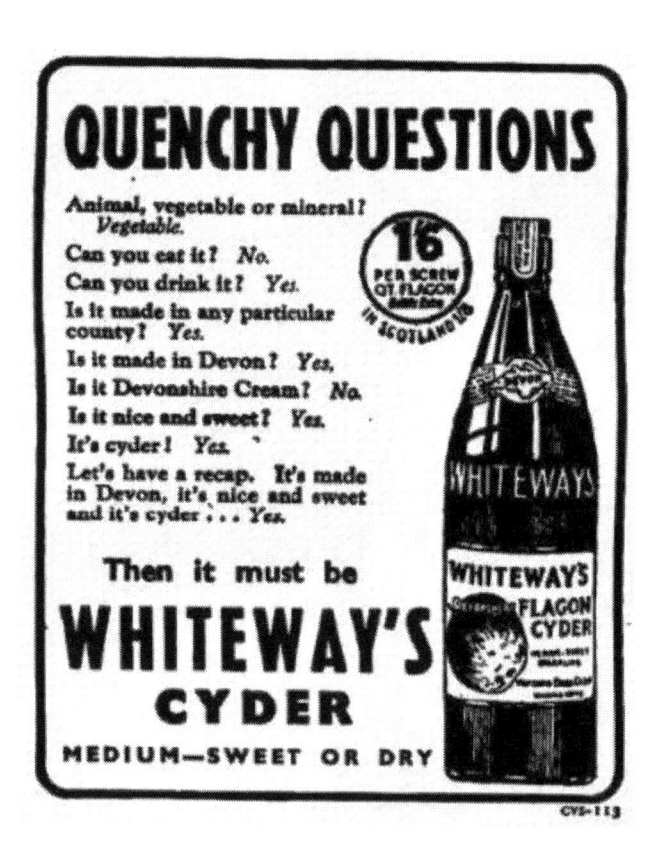

## QUENCHY QUESTIONS

Animal, vegetable or mineral? *Vegetable.*
Can you eat it? *No.*
Can you drink it? *Yes.*
Is it made in any particular county? *Yes.*
Is it made in Devon? *Yes.*
Is it Devonshire Cream? *No.*
Is it nice and sweet? *Yes.*
It's cyder! *Yes.*
Let's have a recap. It's made in Devon, it's nice and sweet and it's cyder... *Yes.*

Then it must be

## WHITEWAY'S CYDER

MEDIUM—SWEET OR DRY

Over in Europe, the Allied decision to make the Western mark sole legal tender in Western Berlin, brought the city's retail trade almost to a standstill. During inquiries at shops, it was found that the only ones doing any business were food shops. However, trade was expected to pick up again after March 31st, when most Western workers would, for the first time, receive a large proportion of their wages in Western marks.

Tourism was a hot topic at the end of the month, when the suggestion that American tourists got "browned off" in London after a few days was made by J. D. Mack in the Commons. The House was debating the question of improving tourism to Britain and how Americans could be made to spend dollars. Mr. Mack said, on the question of entertainment: "When the American comes to London, he stops for two or three days, and then gets browned off, and goes to Paris, which, after all, has something to show and the cafes, are open.

Picked specially for you!
ONLY THE finest GOES INTO
BIG BEN
SQUASHES
R. FRY & Co., Ltd., Ashford Road, Eastbourne

# APRIL

TUCKED away in the back of most newspapers was the story that Faroe Islanders received a Bible in their own language for the first time ever. It had been translated from Danish and printed in the Faroes – sparking a record attendance in Services that month. It was widely remarked that it was nice to read a story about the Faroes which 'didn't concern whale meat'.

But, meat was the big topic, with housewives complaining that butchers' meat 'might be venison or donkey' – making up some of the ammunition taken by members of the United Housewives Association to the Food Ministry when they tried to see the Minister to complain about the "poor quality" of foods, including bread. They also asserted too little tea and sugar was available. Furthermore, they sent a letter to Prime Minister Attlee asking that offers from the Dominions to supply Britain with meat or other foodstuffs, 'shall be accepted in preference to dealing with foreign markets.'

To an extent their concerns were justified. It was reported that a fair amount of beef with black mould was getting into Britain and it was highly dangerous. Authorities instructed that the whole of the meat affected should be cut away and burned. "If there is white, blue or green mould on meat, it is not highly dangerous. The mould can be wiped off and the meat itself will be good. The knife used must afterwards be sterilised," officials said. Then there was the problem of parasites on meat. The government said: "The moral of it all is thorough cooking. There are very few infections that are not killed when food is well cooked". Horseflesh was being eaten far more than was expected, which incidentally, was far less affected by disease than cattle. At the same time, complaints that Tree of Heaven leaves were being used considerably for adulteration of tea continued. Inspectors, it was reported, even found 50 percent of clay in coffee, whilst there were reports of cooking fat which was 'nothing but a mixture of wax and water'. One report complained that liquid paraffin and Vaseline had been used for making tarts.

Rationing had been good for florists – but the good times were coming to an end as possible competition from sweets and chocolates - which the florists feared would follow de-rationing. Florists said they would likely feel the pinch, especially those that had taken up the trade during boom years since 1939.

Members of the Electrical Trades Union employed at Pinewood film studios joined electricians from Denham, who had been on strike. All production at Denham and Pinewood has now stopped, and 2,000 studio personnel sitting idle. The original dispute at Denham concerned the proposal to transfer one man to alternative employment at another studio, where his trade union business would not interfere with production.

On April 13th, a Syrian delegation left for Baghdad to begin what were officially described in Damascus as preliminary talks; for a military agreement with Iraq. Official sources said that Syria was ready to take similar steps for military agreements with any Arab States wishing to conclude them. Meanwhile, on that same day, thousands of Jews arrived in the New City of Jerusalem to celebrate the Feast of the Passover.

Another interesting religious development was that many Pakistanis, making their traditional pilgrimage to the holy places of Mecca planned travelling in modern four engined-airliners. A Pakistan commercial airline, which began advertising this service, said that Muslim pilgrims would be charged £120 for a return flight from Karachi to the Red Sea port of Jeddah.

On April 20th, only a few of Wallace Beery's fellow stars attended his funeral, but 2,500 of his fans, mostly women, were there. Others who attended were the former heavyweight champion, Jack Dempsey, and Louis B. Mayer, head of Metro-Goldwyn-Mayer. Wallace Beery had become known as the screen's good-hearted 'villain'. Fans stood behind ropes outside the brownstone church in Forest Lawn memorial park and heard the service over loud speakers. Elsewhere in Hollywood, Olivia De Havilland, the film actress, who had been confined to bed for more than two months, was "doing very well and has shown improvement," her doctor announced.

The following day, sex equality was again a main point of discussion when the annual conference of the National Union of Women Teachers met in Sheffield. Affirming that women had a valuable contribution to make in local, national and international life, they passed a resolution demanding sex equality for vocational training, equal opportunities for appointments to skilled, professional, executive and advisory posts, and the appointment of many more women to Magisterial benches, government committees and Commissions. In sport, Frank Swift, England's goalkeeper in 18 peace-time internationals, announced he would play his last first-class soccer match for Manchester City at Huddersfield, on May 7th. He announced his retirement at the end of the season. Meanwhile, tributes were paid to author Margaret Baillie-Saunders after she died at her home in St. Leonard's-on-Sea. Her forty novels - written the rate of one year - was the impressive output of her working life.

Across Britain there was unbridled joy –especially amongst children – as sweet rationing ended. A rush to buy saw some shops sold within hours, but it was generally felt that the 'sweet stampede' was only a temporary reaction to uncontrolled buying. Newspapers reported that chocolate was the most popular and several shops exhausted stocks, "although boiled sweets, rock and toffees are still easily obtained. Lollipops were in demand children, whose pocket money seemed unlimited". The

THAT WAS 1949

Cornishman newspaper observed:

> With bulging eyes, mouths and pockets, they competed with each other to see who could eat the most of any particular kind of sweetmeat. Their appetites for normal food will probably not be so healthy for a week or so. Adults too have been buying heartily, and some can be accused of hoarding.

**Nice to have a pretty daughter!**

Must admit Jean stands out beside some of these half-alive girls you see... 'Course I do see that she's properly nourished... Funny her thinking herself too old for cod liver oil, though — what about Dad and me?... Sang a different tune when I told her she might thank the fats and vitamins in SevenSeaS for her trim figure, smooth skin and the gloss on her hair... no need to point out that it helps keep her free of colds as well!

*Can you think as happily about your family's health? Wouldn't they be better for SevenSeaS?*

**SEVENSEAS**
PURE COD LIVER OIL

Farmers from outlying districts and early holidaymakers swelled the crowds of hundreds of Bangor townsfolk who waited from an early hour on April 28th to welcome Princess Elizabeth and the Duke of Edinburgh. It was the first visit of the Princess and her husband to North Wales. The royal travellers journeyed by train from London and with them were Mr Attlee, the Prime Minister, and his wife. That same day, Princess Margaret delighted Naples with her 'easy grace and charm'. It was reported that she travelled motor-launch across the blue waters of Naples Bay to the Isle of Capri. One journalist noted: "From the windows of her green-curtained hotel bedroom, where she spent her first night in Italy, she could look over the bay towards the rocky island 21 miles to the south".

In the British province Schleswig-Holstein in Germany, local children were given presents of sweets for hunting the Colorado beetle- which were blamed for the ruin of many crops. The beetle - also called potato bug - attacked the leaves of potato plants and became the Bain of farmers across Europe.

And finally, staying with agriculture news, smiles were raised when the tale of a Sydney suburban fruiterer made the headlines. He had bought a case of Queensland pineapples, and with it something he had not asked for—an eight-foot non-venomous carpet snake, which came out with the first pineapple. It followed fleeing customers into the street, where it was caught by the fruiterer!

# MAY

RATION starved Britons dribbled on with envy on May 3rd when newspapers reported that the whites of 14,000 eggs and 3,500 whole eggs were used in a four-ton cake made in Miami for a firm's party. One reader was so amazed; that he called the newspaper to check they had not made an error. The figures, he was told, were correct. Ironically, that same day, Paul Henkel, a New York restaurant owner complained that Americans ate too fast. "It's the same all over, from snack bars to hotel rooms. Result: Fifty years ago there were 31 indigestion remedies, now there are 231," he complained.

Meanwhile, the film-world held its breath as troops searching for the teenage French film actress Cecile Aubry - who went missing in floods in south Morocco - were told that she had been sheltering in an Arab village and was being returned to her film party. Tyrone Power and Orson Welles were also marooned but not "missing" and were also back on set, much to the relief of female fans. Across the Mediterranean, an Italian corvette brought Princess Margaret from Capri into Sorrento on the Bay of Naples. Sailors formed a guard of honour as she came down the gangplank with the armful of roses they had given her.

On May 9th, the UN voted overwhelmingly favour admitting Israel to the United Nations in the present session. Voting was 33 to 11, with 13 abstentions, thus ensuring the required two-thirds majority in the Assembly. At the same time, the Israeli Foreign Office received a cable from the British Foreign Office requesting that Mr. A. K. Helm, nominated British Minister to Israel, be given all rights and immunities of a full diplomatic representative. In London, the Secretary for the Colonies announced that the King had approved the appointment of Sir Andrew Barkworth Wright, Governor and Commander-in-Chief of the Gambia, to be Governor and Commander-in-Chief of Cyprus, in succession to Lord Winster.

That same week, the Minister of Food announced that the ordinary weekly domestic cheese ration was increased from 1.5oz. to 2oz. A corresponding increase was made in the allowances to restaurants and hotels. The special cheese ration 12oz. a week and the seaman's ration were not affected. The cheese ration was reduced the previous year because Britain had ceased buying food from the United States owing to the dollar shortage. At the same time, those that bought food parcels from abroad - including the Republic of Ireland – were warned that they rendered themselves liable to prosecution.

In a distraction from rationing, Neville Duke - a test pilot - flew a Hawker Fury plane 1,011 miles from London to Rome in just 2 hours 30 minutes and 58 seconds on May 12th. Duke also knocked 3 hours 54 minutes off the London-Karachi record when he arrived at Karachi soon after to deliver the plane to the Pakistan Air Force. At the same time, the *Lockheed Aircraft Corporation* received orders for 16 additional *Constellation* transport planes from four foreign airlines – the aviation industry in Britain was taking off.

Meanwhile, the tense situation in Berlin – with the Russian blockade over - continued to fester. On May 12th, passengers aboard the first German inter-zonal train to reach the city complained of rough handling by Russian frontier guards. Men, women, and children among the 150 passengers said armed Russian soldiers ordered them off the train when reached the Soviet boundary, searched them and their belongings, confiscated all Western licensed newspapers and magazines, and forced them to change their West German currency. They also said the Russians kept them standing in line for several hours before being allowed to board the train again.

The following day in Britain, the story of a terrible tragedy continued to shock the nation. The accidental feeding of a disinfectant solution to three premature babies at a hospital in Glasgow was the subject of a widely publicised inquiry. It transpired that the babies, who died on March 28th, had been fed a non-poisonous disinfectant solution which was accidentally mixed with breast milk into their flasks.

In London, the Rev. Colin Roberts, secretary of the Home Mission Department of the Methodist Church, announced that for the first time in nearly 20-years the Methodist Church showed an increase in membership.

On May 28th, Britain, the USA, France and Russia met in New York to discuss detailed arrangements for lifting the Berlin blockade and the holding of a meeting of the Council of Foreign Ministers. The announcement was made simultaneously in New York, at the American United Nations' delegation office, and at the State Department in Washington.

In the UK, an expert said it was likely to be some years before atomic stations replace existing power stations, but he was 'absolutely certain' that it would happen and that as a result coal supplies will be conserved. This view was expressed by Prof. M. L. E. Oliphant, head of the atom-splitting team at Birmingham University. There was the possibility of electrical power by atomic energy, but the materials were expensive, he said.

At the cinema, Richard Widmark gave an outstanding performance as a night club owner with a sadistic streak to his nature in the 20th Century-Fox film, "Road House," which was screened nationwide. Also in the cast were Ida Lupino, Cornel Wilde and Celeste Holm. This taut drama told the story of a ruthless schemer who plans a diabolical revenge on his friend and partner who won the love of a girl he wanted for himself. One critic observed: "The film was brilliantly directed by Jean Negulesco, who has kept the tension running at a high pitch throughout".

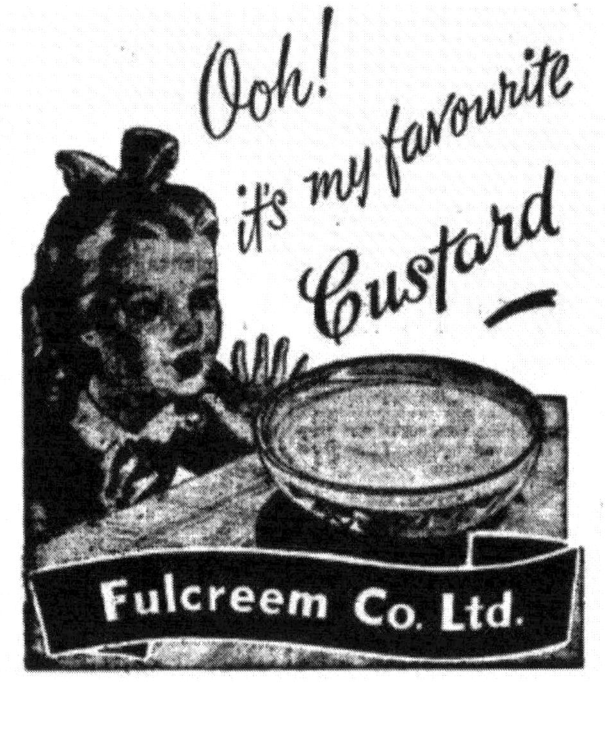
Ooh!
it's my favourite
Custard
Fulcreem Co. Ltd.

# JUNE

THE MONTH began with the publication of encouraging figures showing a reduction in the percentage of schoolchildren requiring dental treatment, with the neglect of treatment due to the war years. In Eastbourne, the senior dental officer reported that 4,414 children had been inspected, and of that number 2,658 or 60 percent, were found to require treatment. This was an improvement on the previous year's figures when 65 percent were referred for treatment, and a still more encouraging figure when it was remembered that in 1946, 85 percent were referred.

Food grumbles continued when cafes and canteens were told they would get no more fresh eggs after July 16th, and cafes which had saved eggs during the past few months will not be permitted to sell them after August 13th. This had been done to prevent speculators buying up eggs for resale. However, the end of restrictions on milk sales was forecast for the following year.

Meanwhile, a clean food campaign, launched by the *British Tourist and Holidays Board*, needed glamorising according to Mr. A. E. Burdett, the chairman of the Board's catering division: "If we can glamorise it in any way we can get a new line on the problem," he said. "This question of washing hands, for example. If, instead of having a lump of soap lying in the wash basin, we had scented soap we might get more people to wash their hands". Sir Alexander Maxwell, chairman of the Board, emphasised the dependence of the tourist trade on adequate catering facilities, and said that the first year of the cleanliness campaign had been a tremendous success. The government had stated that earnings from overseas tourists were expected exceed £40million, plus at least £15million in fares to British companies, and the Government hoped that the total £17.5million would be spent in dollars. These figures were given by Harold Wilson, President of the Board of Trade, during debate the Commons on the tourist and holiday Industry.

Flying at a height of 34,000 feet most of the team American *Shooting Star* jet planes took off from Iceland touched down at Kinloss on June 9th. They covered the distance in just 1 hour and 40 minutes. It was the first occasion on which jets had been ferried by air from America to Germany, and was the first time in history that a mass flight across been made by U.S. planes. The *Shooting Stars* replaced other jet aircraft in Germany and left America on May 25th, but bad weather and repairs held them up at Iceland and Greenland.

At the cinema, audiences were introduced to the delightful Huggett family in Gainsborough's film "Here Come the Huggetts". Jack Warner, Kathleen Harrison, Jane Hylton, Susan Shaw, Petula Clark and Jimmy Hanley were the principal players. The story revolved around the Royal Wedding and dealt with the ordinary happenings of a typical British middle-class household. Drama and comedy, laughter and tears were all combined and formed an ideal mixture.

**Dewar's "White Label" SCOTCH WHISKY**

Maximum retail prices
33/4 per bottle
17/5 per half-bottle
As fixed by
The Scotch Whisky Assoc.

Although small in size compared with the oceans of the world, the North Sea, when in angry mood, can claim the unenviable distinction of being the most dangerous stretch of water of them all to shipping. A fifty-year survey of merchant ships published in early May, reported that abandoned, foundered or missing while trading under peacetime conditions, reveals that 26 per cent, of the casualties occurred during voyages across the North Sea and to North European ports. The North Atlantic accounted for 18 percent. Over the previous fifty years, the total number of sea-going ships abandoned, foundered or missing was 1420, an annual average of thirty eight. Coal was the most dangerous cargo, for no fewer than 386 ships, 27 percent of the total, was carrying coal when lost.

Ironically, days after that report was published, a 2,950-ton Belgian cross-Channel steamer the *Prinses Astrid*, with 218 passengers and crew of 65 aboard, struck a mine and sank 15 miles off Dunkirk. Immediately after the explosion the vessel took on list. She slowly sank, settling back even keel. Only her masts and funnel were visible above the water a few hours after the explosion. Although tugs tried tow her into shallow water she sank before they could succeed.

On June 29th, a jet fighter tore out of the sky at Ipswich in 500 m.p.h. dive and "decapitated" a semi-detached house. The pilot of the fighter, which had been taking part in a mock air battle over the town, was killed. Two children were injured, one critically. The aircraft crashed on to a belt of trees and burst into flames after it had hit the house. Local mothers said they would petition the Air Ministry to put an end to such aerial battles over the town. "All afternoon we had been anxiously watching the mock battles in the sky," said Mrs Thurkettle, a local resident. "The fighters were flying terribly low and making fearful noise."

Meanwhile, American officials were told that Britain would heavily cut her dollar-buying. Commodities chiefly affected will be tobacco, cotton, cheese and timber.

By then end of the month, it was revealed that a start was to be made in using the vaccine known as

B.C.G. as a protection against tuberculosis. The government stressed that this was not form of treatment, or a cure for the disease, but only a method of vaccination that may prevent a person from getting it. B.C.G. vaccination would in due course be offered to all hospital nurses and medical students, as one among other precautionary inoculations. It was also made available to chest physicians that wished to give the vaccine to persons known to be in close contact with someone suffering from tuberculosis.

Finally, the month ended with some good news from Berlin when a new N.A.A.F.I. for airmen and airwomen was opened at the R.A.F. Station at Gatow, the main British terminal of the airlift. The building was a Luftwaffe aircrew cadet mess during the war, and later became a kitchen for German workers employed on the airlift. It was redecorated and contained games, coffee, and writing rooms, a smoking lounge and cafeteria, as well as a bar built resemble a typical English tavern. There is also a shop for service families' and fittings were chromium-plated and the lighting was of 'the fluorescent strip type'.

Acknowledged as one of the finest actresses on the English stage, Dame Edith Evans was proving equally successful in her film career. Her second film, *The Last Days Dolwyn*, presented her in the part of Merri, the God-fearing Welsh peasant woman who dominated the story. One critic gushed: 'Her impression of the simplicity and strength which springs from Merri's contented spirit is a moving experience, all too rare in cinema'. Another hit at the box-office was Passport to Pimlico - one of the brightest comedies to come out of a British studio. It told of how a group of unimaginative, down-to-earth Londoners grappled with the strange discovery that their homes were, in fact, on a patch of foreign soil. An unexploded bomb, set off unintentionally, revealed a hidden vault, crammed with treasure and a fifteenth century Royal Charter which decreed that the estate shall be recognised in perpetuity as Burgundian soil, belonging to the Dukes of Burgundy. Confirmation of this came from an eccentric professor of medieval history, Professor Hatton-Zones—an excellent study by Margaret Rutherford. The residents of Pimlico immediately seized the chance to get away from austerity and restrictions. Goods come off the ration; the public house remained open as long as it liked; shops put themselves on the export lists of English firms; ration books were torn up. But there were snags, of which passports, electricity cuts and customs barriers were only a few. The cast included Stanley Holloway and Raymond Huntley.

# JULY

GERMAN SHIPS could once again sail the seven seas, the Anglo-American joint export import agency announced in Frankfurt. Since the war, German ships had been limited to Brest (France), Britain, Scandinavia and Finland, and to the carriage of German exports and imports of transit cargoes for German ports, with certain exceptions. The new policy was expected enable the opening of liner and freight services to Spain and the Adriatic. Meanwhile, 34 people were arrested in Munich after the largest "black market" raid in Bavaria's history. Most of them were displaced persons.

During the 13 weeks ending July 2nd, 129 persons were killed in accidents in coal mines in Great Britain, according to the Ministry of Fuel and Power published in the "Board of Trade Gazette." One hundred and sixteen deaths occurred underground, the remaining 18 being surface accidents. Men seriously injured in the same period totalled 566.

On July 14th, a bomb was thrown while Indian Prime Minister Pandit Nehru was calling mammoth meeting at Calcutta. One policeman was killed, and five people were injured. The bomb was thrown at police picket guarding the crowd of a million men and women. That same day, figures showed that unemployment dropped by 40,522 over the month ending June 13th to a total of 263,643, the lowest figure for two-years. In July 1947 the total was 255,500. Apart from London, Scotland enjoyed the biggest improvement.

**Ask for ELDORADO**

OLDEST AND BEST KNOWN SOUTH AFRICAN WINE

*A vintage wine of consistent quality and bouquet*

BOTTLE 14/6 • Half Bottle 7/9

*From your Grocer or Winemerchant*
TAWNY AND WHITE

Ironically, the following day, Skyways, one of Britain's largest air charter companies, dismissed 400 of their flying and ground staff. The dismissals were all from Dunsfold Aerodrome in Surrey. Captain R. J. Ashley, managing director of Skyways, said: "The sackings are necessary because of the Government's curtailment the number of civil planes used on the

Berlin airlift. We are withdrawing seven of our eight planes on the airlift at the end of the week".

In the USA, the Steel Workers' Union announced a partial strike. The Union president, Philip Murray, said the strike would operate in those companies which had rejected President Truman's proposal for a 60-day, truce while issues in dispute were investigated.

Meanwhile in Birmingham, granting a decree nisi on the grounds of cruelty to Alfred Aubrey Freestone (38), Mr Justice Barnard said that he could not imagine anything more cruel than to subject a man day after day and night after night, to nagging. The judge said the husband alleged that during the whole of the married life his wife, Mrs Myra Freestone (47), had subjected him to "a constant course of nagging, which finally injured his health". Having seen them both in the witness box, the judge had no doubts whatever in accepting the evidence of the husband and rejecting that of the wife.

The weekend of July 22nd, was one of the heaviest the year for passenger traffic in Britain. At King's Cross additional 14 extra trains entered London, and 12 left for the north. Eastern Region arrangements included more than 60 scheduled relief trains. Nine hundred motor coaches were booked to leave on the Saturday and 800 the following day.

To mark the record-breaking Boston run of the

British film "Rod Shoes"—the Governor of Massachusetts, Paul Dever, held trans-Atlantic telephone conversation with the British film magnate, J. Arthur Rank on July 23rd. In New York, where the film was in its 40th week, tickets were being sold for as far ahead as next January, at double the usual charges. That same day, Tirana radio said that information had reached Albania that the 'Yugoslavs are joining the Monarcho Fascists (Greek Government) for an attack on our country, so as to fulfil the part assigned to them by their Anglo-U.S. masters.' The radio also alleged that Yugoslavs had made incursions onto Albanian territory.

In Sunderland, the Corporation Health Committee was so concerned at the increase in the number of cases of pulmonary tuberculosis among children under 15 - they had almost trebled in the last ten years—that its Emergency Sub-Committee reviewed steps which could be taken to prevent further spread of the disease.

Meanwhile, the regimental band of the Scots Guards, in full dress began a recruiting tour in Scotland playing at Ayr, Kilmarnock, Glasgow and Paisley. A brigade recruiting, team also visited the Scottish Command. During the previous year, only 71 Scotsmen enlisted in the regiment, which was far below- requirements.

# AUGUST

News arrived on August 6th that the death toll from an Ecuador earthquake was reported to be more than 400, with at least 3,000 injured. Many of the injured were not expected to live. Six cities were reported to be in ruins. Rivers reached flood level and were threatening damaged towns. Experts said the entire range of the Andes Mountains had been shaken.

Indian oranges, grapes, sweet limes, peaches and pears were to be 'airlifted to the United Kingdom' with over 6000 lb of hothouse grapes being flown immediately. Export to Britain of grapes, tomatoes and cucumbers were set to continue until January.

A Coalition Government began rule Syria after the execution of President Zaim and his Prime Minister, Dr. Barazi was formed in Damascus on August 15th by Hashem Atassi Pasha, a former President. The New York Times saw in the coup an outward manifestation of the 'revolutionary groundswell' sweeping the Arab World as a result of its defeat by Israel. French Left-Wing papers accused Britain of engineering the Syrian coup d'etat in order to get rid of a hostile regime'.

On August 14th, 73-year-old leader of the Christian Democratic Union was tipped as the first German Chancellor since Adolf Hitler after elections in which there was a heavy swing to the Right. His predominantly Catholic Party won 139 seats in the Lower House of the Federal Republic of Western Germany out of a total of 402 seats —eight seats and 500,001 more votes than its chief opponent, the Socialist Party. His party stands for free commercial enterprise and federal government on the Bonn model as against the highly centralised type on which the Prussianised Reich was built. The French Minister of the Interior, M. Moch, speaking of Germany's proposed admission to the Council of Europe, said that she seems have learned nothing since her defeat.

**FLY** BY REGULAR AIR-LINE FROM **YEADON**

ISLE OF MAN — Saturdays only £7/5/0 Return
(in 1 hour) DAILY SERVICE — Other days £5/16/0 Return

LONDON (in 90 minutes) Monday to Friday £8/16/0 Return

JERSEY (in 3 hours) Saturdays only £16/0/0 Return

Specially reduced fares for Children

AIR CHARTER Anywhere—Anytime
*CHEAP DAY Return fares to race meetings

Enquiries to
LANCASHIRE AIRCRAFT CORPORATION LTD.
YEADON AIRFIELD · · NEAR LEEDS
Telephone: Rawdon 172. Or any Travel Agent
in association with the B.E.A.

The first television transmissions in the Midlands began in Birmingham on August 16th. A mobile transmitter, with normal range of 10 miles, operated for the benefit of the radio trade was in preparation for the transmissions from the Sutton Coldfield transmitter, expected to begin October or November.

The transmitter was working on only 1 kilowatt, compared with the 35 kilowatts of the permanent station.

The following day it was announced that a small quantity of cortisone, the American discovery for the treatment of rheumatic diseases would be made available to the Empire Rheumatism Council for experimental purposes in Britain. The drug was so scarce that only about 20 patients had been treated with it in America.

On August 18th, evidence that a wasp sting could have fatal results was widely reported at an inquest at Mablethorpe on Mrs. Bertha Mary Leggate, 53, who was said to have died within five minutes of being stung on the hand wasp. Henry Leggate said that as his wife was preparing tea for the harvesters when she said "I've been stung again by a wasp. I believe I am going faint. Get me some smelling salts. She died in a few minutes. Some 14 days previously she had been stung by a wasp the other hand but it cleared up in about a week.

Figures showed that unemployment in the Anglo-American zone of Germany reached a new postwar record of 1,267,247 in mid- August, according to the German Bizonal Labour Administration. The figure was 12,699 above that for July 31st.

Meanwhile, former Prime Minister Winston Churchill, who was staying at Lord Beaverbrook's villa near

Nice, contracted a chill while bathing in the Mediterranean. Lord Moran, his physician, who was sent for reported that Mr. Churchill was much better, but would require few days' rest and quiet. Duncan Sandys, who is in Strasbourg, had a talk with Churchill by telephone and found him "in rare form".

**'Granola'**
British Biscuits at their Best
**Macfarlane Lang**

*Made from finest home-grown wheatmeal*
Established 1817

An inquest on twenty-three victims of a B.E.A. Dakota crash at Oldham on August 19th, heard police Superintendent Metcalfe, of Huddersfield, say of the rescuers: "I have never seen a better demonstration of personal disregard in the interests of others. How much suffering was alleviated can never be measured". Only evidence of identification was given. Many bodies were identified by their personal possession and clothes. The inquest on the twenty-fourth victim, Cyril Beenstock, was opened and adjourned to allow the body to be buried in accordance with Jewish rites. The Dakota which carried thirty-two people, including crew, was on a flight from Belfast to Ringway Airport, Manchester. Nobody at the airport, only a few minutes flight away, knew of the crash until villagers sent an SOS for ambulances.

A German Government could make "no greater mistake than to press for hastening Germany's inclusion the Atlantic Pact," Dr. Adenauer, designated first Chancellor of Western Germany, said on August 25th. "Germany must first achieve her inclusion in the European organisation, and in the Council of Europe. Everything else must develop from that," he said.

On that same day, over in New York, a system for broadcasting colour television was announced by the electronics giant RCA. The company said that its system meant that existing black and white television transmitters would be able to send in colour with small addition to existing studio equipment. Furthermore, the Columbia Broadcasting System (CBS) also announced that it had made an adapter which would enable sets to pick up colour broadcasts in colour.

August ended with the U.S. Government labelling 22 more areas of the nation as having a critical employment problem, meriting special federal aid. This increased the list to 32. The Labour Department announcement said that the increase did not itself mean an increase in unemployment, but only that the Government's search for such areas had been wide.

# SEPTEMBER

A THREE-NATION conference on hazards and safety in connection with atomic piles and related subjects began in the United Kingdom. The Ministry of Supply stated that the conference included discussions under the technical co-operation programme of U.S., U.K., and Canada which was established early in 1948. This programme does not include weapons information.

At least 5,000 thirst-crazy elephants, driven out of the parched interior of Kenya towards the coast in a mad search for water, have highlighted the most serious drought in the African Continent for more than a century. The great herds of elephants are crashing across country, trampling down the growing crops, threatening towns and villages in their panic flight and making an already serious food situation even more perilous.

Queensland's butter exports to Britain were the highest for eight seasons, stated the annual report of the Queensland Butter Marketing Board. Exports totalled 1,265,389 boxes, nearly 5,000 boxes more than in the previous season.

Stripped of its technicalities, an announcement of the devaluation of the pound – by 30 percent - meant that the UK's response to the call for harder work and the tightening of belts was not sufficient to enable

Britain to avoid taking a grave and distasteful step. One newspaper noted: "How repugnant the decision must be to the Government is shown by the fact that only two months ago Sir Stafford Cripps was telling us that they had "not the slightest intention of devaluing the pound." The drastic nature of the rate reduction came as a shock.

*INSIST ON Keiller DUNDEE Marmalade – also KEILLER JAMS they're delicious!*

On the 27th, three former women supervisors of the notorious Ravensbrueck concentration camp for women were sentenced to death by a French war crimes tribunal in Rastatt (French Zone). They were Maria Minges Ingeborg Schulz (28). Ruth Schumann (28). They heard the sentence without any sign of emotion. They were found guilty of maltreating camp inmates - as a result of which several French women died. That same day, the bodies of 14 members of the crew were recovered from the wreckage of two Lincoln bombers which collided in mid-air and crashed in flames over Staythorpe, a small village near Newark, as Britain's great air exercise "Bulldog " ended early. When the search was called off because of thick fog, twelve bodies had been recovered from the wreckage.

At the end of September, the remarkable news that Larratt Battersby, a Lancashire ex-hatter, was planning to build a memorial institute to Hitler—in South Africa hit the headlines. He hoped to raise enough money from among the late Fuhrer's admirers to establish a permanent home to further Nazi teachings and beliefs. Mr. Battersby said: "I never met Hitler—but I know him spiritually. Hitler was God-guided and he died a martyr. I plan to make the memorial a centre for a world philosophy based on Hitler's teachings. I shall call it the Adolf Hitler Memorial Institute". Battersby was detained for three years on the Isle of Man during the war because he wanted a negotiated peace with Hitler.

After being trapped underground by a fall of stone for 23 hours, three Thornley Colliery, Co. Durham miners were rescued. The men were George Bowes; Harold Raine (47), and Herbert Mills. They were cut off about a mile from the shaft by the fall and rescue squads, working in relays, had to hack a way through 20ft. of stone to reach them. The men throughout the whole time remained cheerful and in good spirits. After being rescued, they had a bath and went home.

Finally, the eating of a bad sausage roll was held at a St. Pancras inquest at the end of the month. The snack was said to have been responsible for the death of Mrs. Rosalie Dowsing (76), of Newington Green Road, Islington. A daughter said that the roll made on a Friday, was eaten on Monday. A verdict of "Death by misadventure " was recorded.

# OCTOBER

THE 130-ton giant Brabazon airliner flew for over two hours from Filton, Bristol, on October 3rd on high speed tests. A spokesman of the Bristol Aeroplane Company said afterwards that the trials had been "very satisfactory." A few days later, a Federal court in San Francisco sentenced "Tokyo Rose" (Mrs Iva d'Aquino) to 10-years imprisonment and a £3,500 fine for making treasonable broadcasts from Tokyo during the war.

On the 7th, the Soviet-sponsored People's Council met Berlin to proclaim a "German Democratic Republic," Herr Wilhelm Pieck, the 73-year-old Communist was elected President, and announced that a general election would held the Soviet zone October 15, 1950. Russian troops evacuated their central headquarters an the city. The Council met in Goering's former Air-Ministry, which was decorated with huge black, red and gold flags, and banners calling for a "German Democratic Republic for the whole of Germany."

In the UK, the bacon ration was to be increased from 3ozs. to 4ozs. a week for four weeks, and the meat ration from 1/4 to 1/6 a week for three weeks.

Meanwhile, Ceylon intends to establish her own Navy. The British minesweeper *Flyingfish* transferred to the Ceylon Royal Naval Reserve, was renamed the Vijaya after Ceylon's first king and became the new

Navy's first warship.

**When Knights were bold —**

**nights were dark without**

# Crompton

*LAMPS*

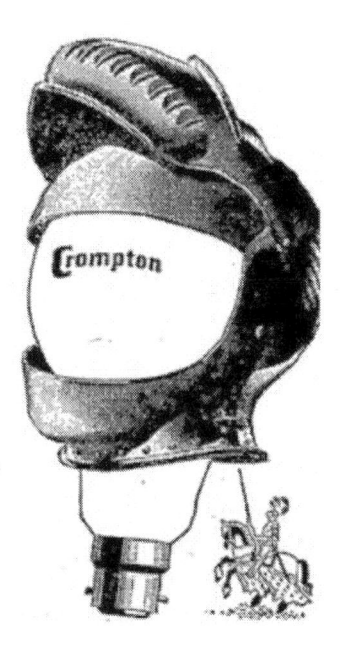

On the 24th, the world celebrated United Nations Day—the fourth anniversary of the United Nations. For a week the U.N. flag was flown in Trafalgar Square and from Government buildings, schools and town halls throughout the country. Arrangements for U.N. Day observances in factories were made by the T.U.C., and special broadcasts were made to schools. New York set the pace for the actual celebrations today, with an open-air ceremony—weather permitting —in the form of a plenary session of the U.N. Assembly at the foot of New York's 42nd Street, in the shadow of the towering framework of the 39-storey structure of the permanent headquarters the

United Nations expects to occupy by 1951.

In other news, it was announced that Britain had received 1,914,705,000 dollars (£683,823,200) worth of food, raw materials, fuel and machinery under the Marshall Plan—more than any other country, the Economic Co-operation Administration stated from Washington.

The search of wreckage of an *Air France* Constellation which crashed in flames in the Azores resumed on October 29th. 48-pople were on board the doomed airliner - rescuers found no survivors. The passengers included boxer Marcel Cerdan former world middle-weight champion, and world-famous French violinist Ginette Neveu. There were no Britons on board. The plane crashed on San Miguel, an island 41 miles long and nine miles wide.

That same day, France laid out a plan for a European monetary bloc at Western Europe's "Economic Cabinet" in Paris. It was believed to advocate eventual merger of France, Italy and the three Benelux countries into one bloc with complete freedom of trade among the members.

It was announced from London that Princess Elizabeth hopes to fly to Malta on Sunday 20th November—the second anniversary of her marriage—to join the Duke of Edinburgh. She planned to make the journey in one of the Vikings of the King's Flight. The Princess will stay with the

Duke's uncle and aunt, the Earl and Countess Mountbatten, at their villa on the island.

## TEA

Under the new regulations. Page 6 from your Ration Book (marked Tea-Tea) must be lodged with your shop keeper,

**not later than JUNE 11th.**

**Be sure you lodge your tea coupons in a shop which sells**

## LYONS TEA

J. LYONS & CO. (I.F.S.), LTD., MARLBORO' ST., DUBLIN

# NOVEMBER

The USA went into mourning after 55 people perished in a mid-air crash between an Eastern Airlines *Skymaster* airliner and a Bolivian twin-engined P3B fighter 'plane over Washington Airport on November 1st, - it was the seventh air tragedy in a week. The airliner was carrying 51 passengers and a crew of four. Only Bolivian ace pilot, Capt. Eric Rios Bridoux, was in the fighter and he was said to be the only known survivor, and suffering a broken back. Both machines were coming in to land, and at the time of the collision America's worst commercial air disaster were only 300 feet up.

A few days later, the Shepherd's Bush Studios, London, were bought by the BBC for television production. The Rank Organisation and the BBC announced jointly that arrangements for the sale had been completed. The studios were closed down on grounds of economy. In 1932, with the advent of the talkies, the studios were enlarged and became Europe's biggest and best-equipped film centre.

The Food Ministry stated that owing to the seasonal rise in milk production the weekly allowance of milk for non-priority consumers would be increased from two and half pints to three pints. The milk allowance to catering establishments would also increase from seven and a half pints to nine pints.

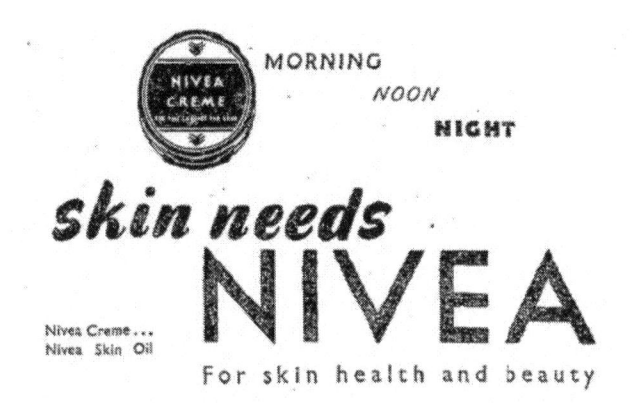

**MORNING NOON NIGHT**

*skin needs* **NIVEA**

Nivea Creme...
Nivea Skin Oil

For skin health and beauty

The Foreign Ministers of Britain, France, and the United States met in Paris for two days to discuss problems of common interest. The three main topics discussed were the European economic situation, relations with the new Western Germany, and the functioning of the Atlantic Pact.

Some of Britain's leading dress and hat designers helped design a new walking-out uniform of the *Women's Royal Army Corps*, which came off the secret list when the models were shown at the War Office. Bottle green was the new colour for the uniforms. The most outstanding change was 'the attractive new bottle-green cap for officers'. It resembled a close-fitting beret at the back, with an upstanding halo effect in front, and a shiny black peak which, for ceremonial occasions, it was edged with gold braid. Other ranks wore large crowned berets.

On the 19th, Prince Rainier - the handsome 26-year-old sovereign of the 370 acre Principality of Monaco— second smallest independent State in Europe—was enthroned. About a thousand people, half the population, stood outside the Royal Palace in pouring rain hour before the ceremony started. The Prince went to the cathedral and mounted the throne last occupied by his grandfather. At the palace, the 80 musketeers of the Monaco Army, the 500 civil servants, and the Bishop swore allegiance. The actual population is about 20,000, mostly wealthy foreigners and habitues of the Monte Carlo casino, Monaco's main source of income.

'Oral'
Shoes for men
have a character that comes of long experience of men's shoe making. They are also comfortable and hard-wearing.
*Ask for them by name.*

Meanwhile, RAF heavy bombers and other British warplanes blasted a terrorist concentration in

Kelantan 60 times in two days in the heaviest attack since the Malayan emergency began. It said that Lancaster's, Beau fighters, Spitfires and Tempest fighters, along with Sunderland flying boats, and Harvard light-bombers hit a camp where terrorists were hiding.

Lucien Dehan, former inspector the Vichy Commissariat for Jewish Affairs, and who denounced more than 400 Jews to the Germans, was sentenced to death at Bordeaux. He told the court on November 20th, "I hate Jews." Elsewhere, Nazi Field Marshal von Manstein slipped in his cell and broke his collar bone. A British Army spokesman said that he was expected to be fit enough to attend court when his trial on charges of committing war crimes was resumed.

# DECEMBER

Presenting Lord Boyd Orr with the Nobel Peace Prize, Mr. Gunnar Jahn, president of the Bank of Norway, said that he had combined scientific knowledge with practical, political insight. "For his work for the cause of humanity, which once begun cannot be stopped, he is worthy of the prize," he said. "However great his scientific contributions, that would not alone have made him worthy the prize. Scientific results create no peace," he said. Lord Boyd Orr had made President Roosevelt's dictum "Freedom from Want" the basis of his efforts towards peace.

Meanwhile, Brooke Claxton, the Canadian Defence Minister, said that Canada had entirely new twin-jet, all-weather fighter, specially developed for use in North American conditions. "It is at present known as the X.C. 100, and is being developed by A. V. Roe (Canada) at Malton, near Toronto," he said. "The engine has been bench tested and hay shown up very; well. The frame will test- flown within a matter of weeks."

The number of live births registered in the great towns of England and Wales during the first week of December was 6,841, compared with 6,938 in the previous week, according to the Registrar General's return.

In cricket, the Australian touring team were all out

for 84 when their three-day match against Transvaal began at Johannesburg. By lunch they had scored 48 for six, Athol Rowan having got all six wickets for 11 runs with off-breaks on sticky wicket. Scores of Test stars included Morris 15, Neil Harvey 7, Miller 7, Loxton 6, and McCool 0. Rowan's final figures were nine wickets for 19 runs.

On the 13th, the Israeli Parliament baulked at a United Nations plan to turn Jerusalem and its surroundings into international State. They voted to transfer the State capital from its present site at Tel Aviv to Jerusalem itself. The Israeli Government thus required additional military protection in Jerusalem, as well as accommodation, which would make it virtually impossible for it to admit any international authority to the area. Both Jordan and Israel had already stated their opposition to the "International State" proposal, and Britain said that the idea was unworkable.

On the 21st, Film actor Clark Gable and (Sylvia) Stanley of Alderley, English widow of Douglas Fairbanks Senior, were married in Santa Barbara, each for the fourth time.

> The lotion is in the lather.
>
> INGRAM'S SHAVING CREAM COMBINES ITS OWN FACE LOTION

Finally, the growing up of Princesses Elizabeth and Margaret, their favourite stories, and their "nursery brawls" were described by their former governess, Marion Crawford, in the "Lady's Home Journal," published in New York. The magazine published "The Little Princesses," her memoirs. In it, the King and

Queen emerge as Papa and "Mummie," two exceptionally domestic parents, and their daughters affectionate, good friends, but both fiery tempered, who "from time to time would set about each other in the good old nursery fashion, no quarter given". Miss Crawford, known affectionately "Crawfie," referred to Princess Elizabeth throughout her childhood nickname, Lilibet.

Printed in Great Britain
by Amazon